BECAUSE I DO

Because I Do

A WORKING MARRIAGE

His Working Documents

Because I Do

Because I Do

A WORKING MARRIAGE

His Working Documents

ONEDIA NICOLE GAGE, PH. D., CLC

BECAUSE I DO

DEDICATION

To all of the married couples who just want a tune-up

To all of the married couples who are in limbo about their future

To all of the married couples who are here because divorce is on the table

To all of the engaged couples who are investigating the concept of marriage

To all of the married couples who are trying it again

BECAUSE I DO

SCRIPTURES

7 Now for the matters you wrote about: "It is good for a man not to have sexual relations with a woman." **2** But since sexual immorality is occurring, each man should have sexual relations with his own wife, and each woman with her own husband. **3** The husband should fulfill his marital duty to his wife, and likewise the wife to her husband. **4** The wife does not have authority over her own body but yields it to her husband. In the same way, the husband does not have authority over his own body but yields it to his wife. **5** Do not deprive each other except perhaps by mutual consent and for a time, so that you may devote yourselves to prayer. Then come together again so that Satan will not tempt you because of your lack of self-control. **6** I say this as a concession, not as a command. **7** I wish that all of you were as I am. But each of you has your own gift from God; one has this gift, another has that.

8 Now to the unmarried and the widows I say: It is good for them to stay unmarried, as I do. **9** But if they cannot control themselves, they should marry, for it is better to marry than to burn with passion.

10 To the married I give this command (not I, but the Lord): A wife must not separate from her husband. **11** But if she does, she must remain unmarried or else be reconciled to her husband. And a husband must not divorce his wife.

12 To the rest I say this (I, not the Lord): If any brother has a wife who is not a believer and she is willing to live with him, he must not divorce her. **13** And if a woman has a husband who is not a believer and he is willing to live with her, she must not divorce him. **14** For the unbelieving husband has been sanctified through his wife, and the unbelieving wife has been sanctified through her believing husband. Otherwise, your children would be unclean, but as it is, they are holy.

15 But if the unbeliever leaves, let it be so. The brother or the sister is not bound in such circumstances; God has called us to live in peace. **16** How do you know, wife, whether you will save your husband? Or, how do you know, husband, whether you will save your wife?

1 Corinthians 7

BECAUSE I DO

A WORKING MARRIAGE: HIS DOCUMENTS

LIBRARY OF CONGRESS

Because I Do: A Working Marriage

His Working Documents

All Rights Reserved © 2022

Onedia N. Gage, Ph. D., CLC

No part of this book may be reproduced or transmitted in
Any form or by any means, graphic, electronic, or mechanical,
Including photocopying, recording, taping, or by any
Information storage or retrieval system, without the
Permission in writing from the publisher.

Purple Ink, Inc. Press

For Information address:
Purple Ink, Inc.
10223 Broadway St., P292
Pearland, TX 77584
www.purpleink.net ♦ onediagage@purpleink.net

Onedia Gage Ministries

www.onediagage.com ♦ onediagage@onediagage.com

ISBN:

978-1-939119-95-7

Printed in the United States

Other Books by
Onedia N. Gage, Ph. D., CLC

Are You Ready for 9th Grade . . . Again? A Family's Guide to Success
As We Grow Together Daily Devotional for Expectant Couples
As We Grow Together Prayer Journal for Expectant Couples
As We Grow Together Bible Study: Her Workbook
As We Grow Together Bible Study: His Workbook
Because I Do: A Working Marriage Her Working Documents
The Best 40 Days of My Life: A Journey of Spiritual Renewal
The Blue Print: Poetry for the Soul
From Fat to Fit in 90 Days: A Fitness Journal
From Two to One: The Notebook for the Christian Couple
Hannah's Voice: Powerful Lessons in Prayer
The Heart of a Woman: The Depth of Her Spirit (Poetry)
Her Story The Legacy of Her Fight: The Bible Study
Her Story The Legacy of Her Fight: The Devotional
Her Story The Legacy of Her Fight: The Legacy Journal
Her Story The Legacy of Her Fight: Prayers and Journal
I Am.: 90 Days of Powerful Words: Affirmation and Advice for Girls
ILY! A Mother-Daughter Relationship Workbook
In Her Own Words: Notebook for the Christian Woman
In 90 Days: What Will You Do?
In Purple Ink: Poetry for the Spirit
Intensive Couples Retreat: Her Workbook
Intensive Couples Retreat: His Workbook
Living A Whole Life: Sermons Which Prompt, Provoke, and Provide Life
Living an Authentic Life
Love Letters to God from a Teenage Girl
The Measure of a Woman: The Details of Her Soul
The Notebook: For Me, About Me, By Me
The Notebook for the Christian Teen
On This Journey Daily Devotional for Young People
On This Journey Prayer Journal for Young People
On This Journey Prayer Journal for Young People, Vol. 2
One Day More Than We Deserve Prayer Journal for the Growing Christian
Promises, Promises: A Novel
Queen in the Making: 30-Week Bible Study for Teen Girls
Queen in the Making: 30-Week Bible Study for Teen Girls Leader's Guide

There's a Queen Within: Her Journey to Self—Worth
She Spoke Volumes . . . And Then Some
Six Months of Solitude: The Sanctity of Singleness Notebook
Six Months of Solitude: The Sanctity of Singleness Prayers and Journal
Tools for These Times: Timely Sermons for Uncertain Times
Walking Tall with a Broken Life
What Did You Say? Affirmations. Encouragement. Motivation.
With An Anointed Voice: The Power of Prayer
A Woman Like Me: A Bible Study
A Woman Like Me: A Daily Devotional
A Woman Like Me: A Sermonic Study
Yielded and Submitted: A Woman's Journey for a Life Dedicated to God
Yielded and Submitted: A Woman's Journey for a Life Dedicated to God An Intimate Study
Yielded and Submitted: A Woman's Journey for a Life Dedicated to God Prayers and Journal

The Nehemiah Character Series

Nehemiah and His Basketball
Nehemiah and His Big Sister
Nehemiah and His Bike
Nehemiah and His Flag Football Team
Nehemiah and His Football
Nehemiah and His Golf Clubs
Nehemiah and Math
Nehemiah and the Bully
Nehemiah and the Busy Day
Nehemiah and the Class Field Trip
Nehemiah and the Substitute for the Substitute
Nehemiah Can Swim
Nehemiah Found the Mud
Nehemiah Reads to Mommy
Nehemiah Writes Just Like Mommy
Nehemiah, the Hot Dog, and the Broccoli
Nehemiah's Family Vacation
Nehemiah's Favorite Teacher Returns to School
Nehemiah's First Day of School
Nehemiah's Sister Moved
Nehemiah's Visit to the Hospital

A WORKING MARRIAGE: HIS DOCUMENTS

BECAUSE I DO

TABLE OF CONTENTS

Great Relationships	21
Equip Your Mate to be Successful	29
Communication = Intimacy	39
How to Save Your Marriage	49
An Amicable Divorce	57
Marriage vs. Technology	63
The Spiritual Diet	73
Forgiveness is Critical	79
Restoration of Trust	84
The Five Love Languages	91
Money Makes a Difference	97
A Successful Second	105
She Started It	113
Fighting Fair	121
Sex: Put It on Her Mind	127
Be a Better Husband	129
Your Time Counts	135
Treat Her Like the Mistress	143

Act Like the Husband	159
Afterword: A Working Marriage	165
Resources	167
The Love Letter Writing Space	168
The Marriage Book List	171
Conference Information	173
Acknowledgments	181
About the Former & Future Bride	183

Dear Participant:

Greetings! Onedia Gage Ministries is a ministry that believes in Jesus Christ. OGM is a non—profit ministry that seeks to support your spiritual journey in all manners possible.

This one-day workshop is designed to meet your needs as an individual as well as a couple. This day is designed to produce results that move your marriage positively and to the next level.

Marriage requires work, every day, no vacations, no breaks—work.

This is new to everyone who is married: the work. But now that we know, we need to be trained to work.

While this one day will not fix all of the 'issues' in your marriage we certainly pray that we can start on the path back to health.

We are glad that you are joining us and looking forward to serving you.

Please bring an open heart and the ability to forgive yourself and your mate.

We invite you to join us for this working workshop. We know that you will achieve some outstanding results.

Please register using the link below:

We look forward to seeing you there!

In God's service,

Onedia N. Gage

Chief Ministry Officer

BECAUSE I DO

GREAT RELATIONSHIPS

What makes a great relationship? How is that defined? Every person defines it differently. That definition had been engrained and fostered your whole life. This definition changes over time as well.

The question is how do you contribute to or contradict that great relationship? Does what you do make it better or worse?

The first take is how each of you defines a great relationship.

How do you define it?

What does your mate say about your definition and vice—versa?

We need to start with the definition of the word so that we will have an idea of where our common ground is and where we differ. Our differences are what we need to understand and manage.

Let's consider our differences. Are the differences severe? One of you does not want to parent children. One of you spends money recklessly. These are major differences. There are minor differences such as how the toilet paper is placed on the dispenser or how many sheets there are in the paper tower roll: half or whole.

How do you define a great relationship? How did arrive at that definition? How long has that definition been forming?

There needs to be a merging of those definitions to create the relationship that you two can function within and be proud of.

That combined definition will function as the foundation of the relationship—which you will grow and develop for years to come—the forever you promised each other.

Once you all reach that definition, then the real work begins.

With that definition, we build a significant, strong relationship.

A great relationship requires daily work. It does not allow for vacations or breaks or days off.

A great relationship means that you consider the other person before yourself. It means that you spend time with your mate. It means that you are concerned about the well-being of the other person. You listen to your mate.

You already know this but the question now is how. How do you keep a relationship great?

WORK. TIME. PRESENCE.

Start with being about to separate what is important from what is minor. Temperatures, toothpaste tubes, toilet tissue rolls, and other such minor items are to be ignored. Buy another toothpaste tube. If necessary, install another toilet paper holder. Decide if the nature of the argument should hold that much influence.

Consider what you spend your time talking about and arguing about. Is it really important? Why don't you spend more time on important topics? What are your deal breakers?

My examples of deal breakers are that he cannot be a smoker, cannot be a cheater, cannot be an abuser of women, and does not demean me. He has to spend time with me authentically. We cannot routinely overspend the budget. These are definite items that will prevent me from progressing in a relationship or cause me to end the relationship.

Great relationships address, manage and solve these issues, or similar ones, on a regular and as-needed basis. Members need to authentically participate in the process.

Great relationships mean that you look forward to coming home, answering the phone, pleasing the other person, and investing in them because they are important to you.

Your commonalities need to outweigh your differences. Your commonalities need to be able to save your relationship from those differences.

Every relationship has a constitution. The constitution is defined as a system of fundamental principles according to which entities are governed. Your relationship has rules and practices, unspoken and written, obvious and understood. Some of these rules will be assumed and others will have to be signed upon and written.

Great relationships also are not temporary. When you are discouraged, you don't quit, nor cause harm in the relationship. Being great also means that you admit when you are wrong and meaningfully apologize.

Great relationships are based on you being great. While no one is perfect, please do remember and behave accordingly so that you are on the same team. On the same team means that you are striving for the same goal, outcome, results, and relationship—one where each person's needs are met and each one craves the relationship.

Being great requires patience, kindness, compassion, love, friendship, like, trust, and some words that I have left out. At any rate, it requires the self that you only break out only for special occasions and sometimes for the wrong people.

Your home is your sanctuary. Home is where you arrive to escape the world, retreat from the chaos, redeem yourself from your errors, and recover from the insults of the world. When you enter that special space, both of you need to remember that the sanctuary is a SANCTUARY. Translation: leave that fighting and chaos outside—both of you.

What is good for the goose is good for the gander. If you can do it, then your mate can too. And don't be surprised when they do. Don't bring chaos where you live. Someone has to stop that chaos or both of you will answer the chaos with additional drama. Unfortunately, no one ever remembers who started it, and no one takes the initiative to stop it. The other person simply needs to cooperate and stop it.

Great is a decision. Mediocrity is also a decision but is usually a result of inaction or lack of motivation. Whatever your 'reason,' it is a destroyer of the relationship. Be great! Surprise! Stimulate! Be proactive! Be active. Start the greatness. Be the reason that greatness happens. Be the reason that you remain married because you exerted the extra energy to make the relationship secure and exciting. Be the person who outdoes the other person, not because it is a competition but because you still want to woo their heart and amaze their soul. Recreate your best dates and your best memories so that you can renew the chemistry in your relationship.

Greatness does not materialize out of thin air. It happens because of work—hard work that does not seem to have an end date or a refill package. Be great. Inspire your mate to be great.

Notes

NOTES

QUESTIONS

1. What is your definition of a great relationship?

   _____
   _____

2. What is the ideal way to reach that definition?

   _____
   _____

3. How do you hold yourself accountable for contributing to a great relationship?

   _____
   _____

4. How do you help your mate with keeping focused on a great relationship?

   _____
   _____

5. How do you measure how well your relationship is progressing?

   _____
   _____

6. How do you keep your relationship healthy such that you look forward to spending time with your mate?

___

___

___

Reflection

EQUIP YOUR MATE TO BE SUCCESSFUL

Intel.

Information.

Maps.

Philosophy.

Idiosyncrasies.

Pet peeves.

Dreams.

Goals.

Past.

Present.

Future.

Location of all skeletal remains.

The Good.

The Bad.

The Ugly.

The tools.

The insight.

The secrecy.

The keys to success.

Every relationship is a combination of two people with varied cultures, experiences, rules, philosophies, boundaries, and idiosyncrasies. These two different people come together for several different reasons to become one unit—a couple. This is like two different companies coming together but they do very different things. They have just enough in common to consider it a great idea but until you get into all of the work of merging, you did not calculate all of the possibilities of the difficulties and differences.

Your mate needs you to open up the vault and share. This is how you equip your mate to be successful. Your mate does not know some of the 'what' that makes you tick and they certainly do not know the why behind your actions and beliefs.

Sharing that information equips them to be successful. Your mate's security is critical for the success of the relationship. These little details become important when they do not understand something that they should and you become frustrated.

The second point regarding security is your mate knowing what other mates (past relationships) know about you. People are not always well-meaning. Imagine if your ex and new mate are in a room together and your ex decides to challenge your new mate on some relational facts. How do you believe that your mate will respond to this situation? We all know that there are a series of consequences for such an event.

The feeling of embarrassment overrides all reasoning. How can you prevent that from happening? Well, sharing usually solves this. Tell your mate whatever it is that could be shared which would destroy the precious nature of your nature.

Stop waiting for your mate to fail. Then you make unforgivable, unretrievable statements that cause your mate to question your intentions, their love, your love, their competence, and then the questions of your future loom over your partner's head. This is a DANGEROUS place. When your mate starts to question the quality of the relationship including the necessity and benefits.

Tell your mate the answers to your questions and the solution to your puzzles and the key to your tests. Make it easy to be in that relationship with you. We all have chosen to be where we are and we could easily choose to be somewhere else. At least half of us do. Why do the other people stay?

Sure, each couple has some differences but are these differences worth dying alone wishing that you had not dismissed her, quit him, or run her away based on something as trivial as the trash or something as important as the time that needed to be spent?

If they have proven themselves as a worthy partner, then put the tests away and stop keeping score. Give them the tools to help them to make you laugh, smile, blush, and reach your intimate and emotional peak. Do it without consequence. Do it because you want your relationship to work. Do it because you want peace and cherish happiness. Do it because you want a comfortable environment.

Remember this is reciprocal as well. Help the other mate to be important to you so that they do not seek affirmation in the presence of others.

Why do you keep your mate at your arm's length and theirs? The distance is not good. This distance is not productive for your overall relationship. Distance attracts distractions and creates divisions and discord and dis-ease and usually ends relationships. This is preventable. Equipping your mate means that they can be successful. Stop testing them. Stop allowing them to fail. Stop creating obstacles to your heart. Stop being difficult on purpose. Stop being cantankerous just because you are too scared or too scarred to let your guard down and let him in completely.

Everyone had rules and boundaries. Everyone has standards and rules. What of these can be relaxed or revised so that you can accommodate your mate? Why are you still holding him hostage for what the last the ex-husband did? What stops you from offering them the tools they need to be successful with you without a cost?

There was a couple who was dating. She wanted to sample living with him and suggested that they try it for two weeks. He declined. He stated that they weren't ready. She asked again a few months later, he declined again. She mentioned it again for a weekend. This time he said maybe but never consented to it happening. A few months later, she was buying a home and it was not going to be ready when her lease was ending. There would be a few days between the lease and the home sale closing that she would need somewhere to reside. He did not offer when she mentioned it. Instead, he asked her if was she going to stay in a hotel. She said no; as a matter of fact, she said, I am going to stay at a friend's house. He was upset. She was surprised.

After three requests and declines, why would she believe that he would say yes? Why would she want to stay there? After all, he was never welcoming before about the idea. This 'emergency' situation does not change the rules, nor should it.

When you are invested, present and offer your time to your mate, they expect that same investment, presence, and time.

That incident spoke volumes about their relationship. Needless to say, this was a severe situation. Their relationship will never be the same.

He held those boundaries tightly. She was not equipped to be successful. Maybe he was not equipped either, and she wanted to be and for them to be successful.

Certainly, this couple is just an example but they do offer you an opportunity to consider how you can best/better consider your mate and their needs and requests. You can also look better at your requests and boundaries to see if you are causing your relationship some stress.

Equipping him to understand you makes it easier to be in that relationship.

Equipping requires time and honesty. You have to want to be available and willing to let him in and put your guard down.

Notes

Notes

Questions

1. What does your partner know?

_____
_____
_____

2. How does your partner know what you need, like, want, and desire?

_____
_____
_____

3. Is there anything that others know that your partner does not? How would that make you feel if you did not know something about your mate that someone else could share?

_____
_____
_____

4. Why are you hesitant to share the facts, and other details so that your mate can be successful?

_____
_____
_____

5. What does your partner need to know?

_____
_____
_____

6. If you love your mate, why do you make it difficult for your mate to be successful?

7. What do you want your mate to do differently to share their authentic feelings with you?

8. What happened if you and your mate fail because you withheld the tools? Which could have been instrumental in insuring success?

REFLECTION

BECAUSE I DO

Communication = Intimacy

Your relationship started with a conversation, a glance, a touch—something started it. Your conversation started with some type of dialogue. It evolved into several other mechanisms: texts, emails, glances, stares, touches, and silence.

When I know what is on your mind and heart then we will grow closer—closer to being one rather than two. This oneness leads to closeness—intimacy. Intimacy is essential to maintaining and growing the relationship.

What happens when there is no intimacy? The relationship does not have a path forward. It becomes dark and desolate. When intimacy is absent, then affairs result and other events separate you two.

What prevents you from communicating? Fear? Boredom? Irreconcilable differences? Difference? Indifference? Love? Hate?

What do you communicate about? Marriage material? Life? Dreams? Feelings? Anger? Conflicts? Plans? Desires? Worth? Achievements? Failures?

Whatever you choose to converse about, you are conversing with the only person that matters in your life—your mate.

What is most important? Conversation with your mate or other events or people? This is your mate—your chosen companion. The one person who wants to hear your triumphs and troubles, pleasure and pain, opportunities and obstacles, achievements and aches, beliefs and bewilderment, decisions and dedications, love and listlessness, is your mate. Also, your compliments and complaints, ideas and indifference, deals and deal breakers.

Let's talk about what to talk about: the best life that you can have together. Decision trees are popular to decide on matters which need to be decided—important, life-altering matters.

Intimacy is an investment in the other person and your relationship.

Your day. Your thoughts. Your needs. Your wants. Your dreams. Your discontent. Your desires. Your love. Your fears. Your sins. Your forgiveness. Your grudges. Your insecurities. Your determination. Your creativity. Your idiosyncrasies. Your anger triggers. Your memories. Your bucket list. Your everything.

Your mate should know more about you and your particular details than anyone else. This is usually a sign of the disconnect between a couple, then this causes other issues between the couple.

Is what you are not willing to share hurting your relationship? Communication will kill or revive your relationship. This will be key to your success or failure.

What does great communication look like, sound like, and feel like? Why is communication difficult? Why can't you be transparent with your mate?

Communication creates trust. This trust sustains your relationship. Communication settles anxiety and provides peace. Communication bridges the gap between where you are in your relationship and where you need to be. Imagine being able to sit next to your mate and share with him your innermost thoughts without fear of judgment, guilt, or shame, rather an acceptance and support. The outcome of that conversation is what draws you two together. It is what keeps you during the ROUGHEST times. It is what keeps you close—so close that nobody can interrupt your relationship. Communication brings your initial interaction and attraction back to your remembrance. Sometimes, you will forget why you love or even like your mate. You need to communicate to remain in an emotional connection with your life partner.

Communication is the place where you ride together and grow together.

Keep the lines of communication open because you are each other's soft place to land. Your relationship should be your safe place, your sanctuary. I have a rule that the outside world and noise should not sound like the inside of my home.

Being transparent requires courage. Sharing your truth can be difficult. But not being supportive or supported is also difficult.

Intimacy is not about sex. Sex is a bonus, because of good communication.

Communication also ensures that emotional monogamy is maintained.

Keep each other talking, seeking solace in each other, and being dependent on each other.

Communication helps each of you accept the growth of the other. Relationships suffer when growth happens and when that growth is a surprise or unwelcomed. Sharing new interests and new dreams is essential to remaining connected with each other.

Communication does not mean solving and fixing. Listening is required. Listen with your heart. Then listen with compassion. Then after the other person finishes, as if you can help, and if so, what can you do? Men are notorious for 'fixing' what a woman is just talking about rather than asking what her intentions are to solve her problem.

You and your mate will define communication differently. Address those differences and address your needs so that you can reach a common ground. One of you does not like to talk while the other one cannot stop talking. Make sure that you are communicating.

The success of your relationship depends on your intimacy and communication.

Would your marriage be different if you had a house phone?

There was a woman who was facilitating a class on marriage so this question came up. Marriages were different when there was a house phone rather than a cell phone. There was still cheating however it was a little more difficult and required more creativity than now. This is the issue that most marriages must overcome.

A marriage is based on and built on trust. Having a cell phone means that trust can be challenged. There are many relationships going on behind the walls of the cell phone and the medium of social media.

What would your marriage be like if you could exchange passwords for all of your devices and applications? What could you achieve if you were honest about your feelings and needs?

Take a chance and be authentic about your total perspective.

NOTES

NOTES

Questions

1. Why is it hard to communicate?
   _____
   _____
   _____

2. What could be better about your current communication?
   _____
   _____
   _____

3. What do you do well in your communication with your mate?
   _____
   _____
   _____

4. What do you need to improve in your communication with your mate?
   _____
   _____
   _____

5. Is your mate jealous of anyone that your talk to more than your mate? Why? What can you do to improve that perception?
   _____
   _____

6. What do you need to do to make sure that you keep you communication strong?

_____
_____
_____

7. Does your intimacy suit your needs? If no, then what can be done to improve that intimacy?

_____
_____
_____

8. Do you and your mate define and judge that intimacy similarly? What can you do to be more aligned?

_____
_____
_____

9. What do you need to share that you have not shared with your mate that you should?

_____
_____
_____

10. How do you forgive your mate for the previously held secrets that were shared/discovered?

_____
_____
_____

11. When can you share all parts of your phone and social media, including direct messages and photos?

_____

_____

_____

12. When will you stop entertaining people on social media?

_____

_____

_____

Reflection

BECAUSE I DO

HOW TO SAVE YOUR MARRIAGE

Why does your marriage need saving? What did you do? What did your mate do? How did the damage start? What does it take to stop the damage? Do you want to remain married? Is your marriage worth saving? Is this the first occurrence or the straw that broke the camel's back? Do you want to save your marriage?

That is the first decision that needs to be made. Is the situation more important than the union? Can the relationship be resilient enough to survive the issues that have impacted your relationship?

The second question is how do we heal from the event which caused the trouble which could have, and maybe actually, derailed your relationship? The third question is can you completely forgive your mate <u>and</u> move forward without regret, resentment, and rehearsing the situation repeatedly in your heart and mind daily?

The fourth question is how can we reunite and that situation NEVER happen again. You may not agree with these statements but you should agree that these are necessary steps.

What happened? What led us here? Who's to blame? The basis of problems that created division within your marriage is a disconnect. How can you solve the disconnect? What reignites the chemistry?

People will offer advice that is solicited and unsolicited; advice that works and will not work. The path that you take is your choice, but you will need to make a choice: to save or not to save.

As a divorcee, you should ask yourself do you want to co-exist without the other person. I don't regret the choice. But if you think that you are going to miss or regret or reconcile, then don't leave. Stay. Fight. Work through. Resolve. Reach a place.

Let's assume that you are reading this and have decided to save your relationship.

The next step is to become emotionally naked in front of your mate. You both need to share completely and transparently with each other. Tell him how you feel about what has happened. Tell him why the incident happened, expressing your remorse, and your desire to reconcile. Please share everything. This is not the time to monitor or manage your thoughts and feelings. That may be what the problem is—not being transparent.

Share the why. Stop keeping details from your mate. Share more with your mate. Remember to treat your mate's information with priority. Healing will happen in several ways: counseling: individuals, and couples, a marriage retreat, the forgiveness of yourself and your mate, and a rededication to your union and to your mate.

Healing is a process that includes allowing yourself to heal. Healing involves a willingness of spirit and heart. Healing does not foster a secure platform: you cannot heal based on 'this' never happening again. Healing is a necessary requirement but will be difficult.

The next step is **not** replaying, rehearsing, and repeating the incident over and over again. You need to stop thinking about the event which led to you here. This is extremely difficult. You cannot allow that to reside in the back of your mind and heart which is available to become front of mind, which then stops all progress, and may even cause your relationship to take a step back.

This can never happen again. Deciding to save the marriage, the healing process, and giving complete forgiveness requires that this does not happen again. EVER. The spouse who was the offender needs to also understand that your behavior must change so that the trust can be rebuilt.

A counselor will tell you both that you each have to overcome and survive this situation. One of you is still skeptical about your words and whereabouts. The other of you is trying to survive the looks, comments, and shame associated with the incident.

Things that will bring your closer:

Honesty. Transparency. Loving. Forgiving. Trust. Partnership. Closeness. Proximity. Dating. Communication. Cooking together. Time.

Depending on how intentional you both are about the progress, you will need to be patient for results. You need to be honest with each other about your feelings and thoughts.

Your mate needs to feel important. Make sure you both indulge the other in their favorite things. This will be difficult but worth it.

Find a couple who can mentor you. It is a seasoned couple that you can meet with and confide in who will offer sound advice for your daily married life.

NOTES

Notes

QUESTIONS

1. What does it mean to save your marriage?
   _____
   _____
   _____

2. Was it one event or a compilation of events that led to this?
   _____
   _____
   _____

3. What does your mate need to do to win you back?
   _____
   _____
   _____

4. Are you a grudge holder? Are you going to make your partner work harder to win you back?
   _____
   _____
   _____

5. Are you willing to hear what your spouse needs in order to make this work?
   _____
   _____
   _____

6. How do you intend to make sure that this does not happen again?

_____

_____

_____

7. What does your reconciliation look like? How will you reach the best relationship space for you and your mate?

_____

_____

_____

REFLECTION

BECAUSE I DO

AN AMICABLE DIVORCE

The ability to divorce the same way in which you came together: with love. It is possible to have an amicable divorce. Make it happen. You two can come together and determine how to split your belongings and finances. Remember that you once loved each other. If you have children, they will judge you based on how you treat each other.

Hire a mediator or have your attorneys meet with you both so that you can create a plan where you can walk away without stress or frustration. Plan to be cooperative no matter how hurt you are based on why you are divorcing.

Amicable saves money and time. Create the best possible scenario for each of you.

Notes

NOTES

QUESTIONS

1. What makes divorce so ugly?
_____
_____
_____

2. Why is this necessary?
_____
_____
_____

3. What can you do to stop the divorce?
_____
_____
_____

4. What can you do to end the marriage in such a way as not to add to the pain of the two of you?
_____
_____
_____
_____
_____

REFLECTION

BECAUSE I DO

Marriage vs. Technology

What happens when the phone rings on your spouse's phone? Does it depend on the time of day? Does it make what you all are doing when the phone rings? Does it matter if the phone is turned so that you cannot see the screen and the caller id? Does it matter if the spouse goes to a different room to speak in hushed tones?

Does it make you nervous or concerned? Is there a reason there may be some distrust? Does your mate know what that call does to you? Are you willing to share your concerns with your mate in a non-accusatory manner so that your mate addresses your actual concerns?

There are real issues and real concerns. A couple teaches a course on marriage and she confided that she did not understand why the younger generation of married couples. The truth is that the couple was married when there was no cell phone. If someone wanted to call either her or her husband, that person had to call her home or their respective workplaces.

Upon that thought, she considered the reality of the truth. This includes emails, social media, and other avenues of technology. As it was a surprise to you, it could be a problem in your marriage. How do you handle that? How do you ensure that your mate feels secure with your use of a cell phone and social media?

If this is the difference between a healthy marriage and a difficult one, then what will you do to insure a healthy marriage? Obviously, your mate will feel more confident and secure if you share and communicate the information regarding the phone calls and social media information, then share it accordingly. The other instance is openly sharing any contact that is made from an outside/unwelcomed source. If you are being flirted with or propositioned in your messages or by other mechanisms, then you need to consider the best way to protect your relationship and the esteem and security of your mate. The other detail is if there is any distrust from the past then this will only add to your already muddled foundation.

Consider how you would feel if it were you who were insecure about your mate's phone and social media activity?

The couple should establish norms—rules—so that each person is respected. Establish times when the phone is off limits and the device-free times during your day or date.

Also, consider the exchange of passwords, and the implication of the understanding of non-misuse of the passwords.

Some things are simple and common courtesy: 1.) Leave your phone face-up. 2.) Don't hide the phone or keep it out of site. 3.) Share your social media information.

There will be people who object to the overall concept but the underlying question would be 'is your mate more important than all others?' Your mate may not feel that way. The point is how to insure that they do feel that way.

After insecurity, the next area that needs and deserves your protection is your time. Couples always need more time. If you spend time—extensive time—on the internet, then could you be spending some of that time with your mate? Relationships require a lot of everything and time is at the top of that list.

You and your mate are together. The relationship deserves your attention and respect—your attention and your respect.

Your mate fought through the whole world to get to you. And if the mutuality is true, then so did you. Because of all that effort, then maybe exerting more would be appropriate and give this relationship what it needs to survive and thrive. If this is too hard, then is the relationship worth it? Is your mate worth it?

The work in a relationship should not be derailed by an unintentional or even an intentional lack of judgment, such as the wrong phone call or an improper text message.

Our daily lives are demanding and toxic, lack of fulfillment or are filled with demise. Our relationships should not be the same. The inside of our homes should not sound the same as our outside world.

Consider the message that you send when you have a password on your phone, no picture on your lock screen, you are not friends on social media with your mate, and every time your phone rings you cannot answer your phone in your mate's presence.

Consider what would happen if you and your mate transferred your phones to a house phone without caller identification. What happens when you answer the phone not knowing who is calling? Can your relationship sustain this exercise?

Notes

Notes

QUESTIONS

1. What do you do to ensure that your mate is secure with social media images, and messages?
   _____
   _____
   _____

2. How do you communicate your insecurities to your mate about technology issues or social media?
   _____
   _____
   _____

3. Why do you feel that way about your mate's behavior?
   _____
   _____
   _____

4. What can your mate do to regain your trust and confidence?
   _____
   _____
   _____

5. What will both of you do to propel the relationship forward?
   _____
   _____

6. Can you and your mate agree on a time to be technology free to review the nuances of your relationship?

_____

_____

7. How does the phone ringing of your mate's phone make you feel?

_____

_____

8. When did you start to feel this way? Did you share this with your mate?

_____

_____

9. Does it depend on the time of day?

_____

_____

10. Does it worsen based on the behavior and the follow up of the details of the call/interaction?

_____

_____

11. Does how you feel cause you to question the relationship?
___
___
___

12. Are you willing to share your feeling in a non-accusatory manner so that your mate can understand how you truly feel?
___
___
___

13. Can you answer and address the needs and concerns, feelings, and thoughts of your mate honestly and openly; offering compassion and understanding?
___
___
___

14. Does this issue cause you to question your mate's commitment?
___
___
___

15. What did you learn? How will you use this information to be a different mate?
___
___
___

16. How will you use this new information that you have access to how to reshape your views and values to propel your relationship forward?

_____

_____

_____

Reflection

BECAUSE I DO

THE SPIRITUAL DIET

What does your marriage require from you spiritually? Should you pray over her daily? Should you pray for him daily? Should you attend church together weekly? Should you fast together on big issues within your lives? What does your marriage require?

There is a connection that keeps couples connected. You need more than a good conversation, good looks, and great sex to keep your marriage healthy. You need to consider how that is developed and how it is sustained.

There are two philosophies: one with a spiritual connection and one without. Each position has its own argument. Each one of them is valid to the person making it.

Consider how you keep focused on your purpose and your plans. Use the spirit which helps guide you and lead you. What does that Holy Spirit say to you?

Based on your foundation from your family, what do they say about your spiritual expectations? Based on your family dynamics, then you should consider what they do for you in order to maintain your relationship's health.

How will you add the spiritual diet to your marriage? Can you keep your marriage focused on the spiritual foundation? When will you submit and recognize the benefits of the connection that produces chemistry so that you can sustain it?

Prayer is necessary for some, while others request prayer but something will happen.

Pray.

Study.

Fast.

Essential for spiritual growth and grounding.

Notes

NOTES

QUESTIONS

1. What does your marriage require from you spiritually?

   _____
   _____

2. Should you pray over him daily? Should you pray for him daily?

   _____
   _____

3. Should you attend church together weekly?

   _____
   _____

4. Should you fast together on big issues within your lives? What does your marriage require?

   _____
   _____

5. What does that Holy Spirit say to you?

   _____
   _____

6. Can you keep your marriage focused on the spiritual foundation?

7. When will you submit and recognize the benefits of the connection that produces chemistry so that you can sustain it?

Reflection

FORGIVENESS IS CRITICAL

When you are wrong, then you apologize—a sincere statement that offers comfort and peace for both parties.

Forgiveness frees you, not the other person. When you forgive, you let your burdens go. You cannot live free if you are withholding forgiveness and holding grudges. This is not healthy for your soul. Your mate needs your forgiveness from time to time. Some events will require more forgiveness than others.

You will want to be forgiven as well. Forgiveness will build the relationship and it affirms the relationship. Forgiveness is not a gift. Forgiveness will afford you the peace that you need to move forward.

Forgiveness is not always easy and it sometimes requires much effort.

Seek peace at all times. Attempt to offer peace to your mate. Forgiveness is ongoing. Not a one-time event.

You will forgive for different reasons, in different seasons, and with a different mentality every time. With a different heart, you will forgive. Hopefully, you will be able to forgive with zeal, without numbness. Hopefully, your need for forgiveness and your ability to forgive won't be met with disdain and numbness.

Keep focused on the health of your relationship via forgiveness.

Forgiveness is a powerful mechanism for continuing to help to repair and grow your relationship. Your relationship has sustained some damage and would have ended without authentic forgiveness. Now that your relationship is in a position to heal, you will need to stop doing the events which require you to need forgiveness.

Your mate is not going to forgive you repeatedly. Keep in mind you need to be conscious of how you would respond if your mate repeatedly needed forgiveness.

Forgive and be forgiven.

Please don't abuse the forgiveness. If not, it will stop.

You cannot maintain a healthy relationship without forgiveness.

If you can't forgive willingly, then there is no need to forgive.

NOTES

Notes

QUESTIONS

1. How long will you need in order to forgive your mate?

   _____
   _____
   _____

2. How long do you need in order to ask for forgiveness?

   _____
   _____
   _____

3. How many incidents do you feel that your mate will be able to endure before you are no longer forgiven?

   _____
   _____
   _____

4. How do you repair what needs to be forgiven?

   _____
   _____
   _____

Reflection

RESTORATION OF TRUST

When you made 'that' decision, did you intend to blow your life up? When you made that choice, what did you think would happen? What could you have done instead? Why wasn't there a dialogue before you made that 'choice'?

Did you consider the long-term consequences? Did those consequences matter?

What does your mate mean to you? If your mate means that much to you, then why do what will hurt that person? Did you believe that you would get away with it? Why?

What happens if that happened to you? Would you be willing to forgive and restore the trust that is needed to continue a healthy relationship?

You want to be trusted and you want to trust. In order to do that, there needs to be dedication and commitment.

You need to attempt to recover and restore your relationship. This requires more intentional communication, consistent accountability, and the elimination, of the threat to your relationship. Be prepared and willing to answer ALL questions. Multiple times. No matter how tired you are of answering the questions. Keep talking. Keep affirming your mate. Keep answering the questions and keep focused on the repair. Change your behavior. Change your patterns. Change your environment. Nothing needs to remain the same.

Be prepared to share your personal effects, such as your passwords, texts, emails, direct messages, and social media information. At any time. For any reason.

Building trust is not optional. The alternative is that your mate walks away. This is when the phrase between a rock and a hard place comes in handy. Extreme measures are required when building trust.

Communication is critical too. Suppose that you cheated. Now, you are trying to recover from this situation. So, you need to decide how you will do that. How do you do that? One way is to become transparent. Meeting the needs of your mate is the second way. Your mate has been asking for some things which you have not relinquished—it is time to do so.

Ask your mate what is required to gain their trust, then do what they say.

Diligence is also needed. You cannot get weary while you are building trust.

Trust is hard to regain. It is similar to saving money. It happens a little at a time. Over a long period of time.

NOTES

Notes

QUESTIONS

1. What was more important than retaining your partner's trust?

___

___

2. Was the event worth what it has cost you?

___

___

3. What is required to restore that lost trust?

___

___

4. How long is required for the trust to be restored?

___

___

5. What are you going to do to help your mate be comfortable again?

___

___

Reflection

THE FIVE LOVE LANGUAGES BY DR. GARY CHAPMAN

When I first read about the five love languages, I could not help but get excited. They are quality time, acts of service, physical touch, giving of gifts, and words of affirmation.

Quality time is the time you spend with others that are important to you. This is a screen-free time with your mate so that you can talk and laugh. About the life that you want. Or your needs.

Acts of Service are doing things for your mate. This is when your mate washed your car or prepares your lunch without you expecting it or asking. Acts of service are also when you cook your mate's favorite meal. This is a gift that cannot be measured. Certainly, your mate could have been doing anything else other than things for you. Please be appreciative.

Physical Touch is hugs and hand-holding. This is not directly about sex, but rather the intimacy that leads up to sex. Some people need the proximity of touch to affirm their closeness.

Giving of Gifts is based on what your mate wants to give you. They give gifts to bridge the gap between the two of you. They express their love through gifts. They may not be the gifts that you wanted but rather what your mate wanted you to have.

Words of Affirmation are the words from your mate which affirm, praise, and close the distance in your relationship. These words will express how they feel about you and consequently how they relate to you.

Most people love in their love language until they understand how to determine what their mate's love language is. Once you learn your mate's love language then you can love them the way they like to be loved and vice versa.

It will change your love life when you love them in their language. It is what they understand.

Try to understand your mate's love language. That information will enhance your relationship.

Notes

NOTES

QUESTIONS

1. What is your love language? Take the quiz.

   _____
   _____

2. What is your love language? Were you surprised?

   _____
   _____

3. What is your mate's love language?

   _____
   _____

4. How hard will it be to change how you approach your mate based on this new information?

   _____
   _____

5. How often should you take this quiz in order to insure that nothing has changed?

   _____
   _____

6. What did you learn about yourself during your lesson?

Reflection

MONEY MAKES A DIFFERENCE

Have you ever heard that money is the root of all evil? Money does not need to be the root of any evil. Consider that money management need to be practical.

What happens if you have one account? What is different about separate accounts?

Arguments about money can seem to cause people to be defensive. Money is earned, so when you squander your assets, you are being foolish. Now that there are two of you, you cannot squander the money. Money is an instrument to acquire your needs. Using money responsibly is a necessity for a successful relationship. When finances are tight or you cannot afford some of the things that you want to buy because the other person overspends, then there will be tension and friction. This is not a comfortable place to be.

There need to be some ground rules about spending money. There needs to be an amount that is a maximum to spend without mutual consent. There needs to be a list of items that are the goals for what needs to be acquired for the household. That is what keeps each party focused on what happens next. This is also a way to not spend money on what you don't need.

Money also speaks to discipline. Everyone has a spending plan that they need to adhere to so that we can save in order to buy bigger items.

It has been suggested that every couple have a monthly meeting about money and other financial information. There need to be financial goals that you put in place so that you can achieve the level you desire.

This is also the time when you will discuss your career, along with possible career changes. Education would also be discussed.

Money is a serious matter. It can fuel or end your relationship. The divorce rate is fueled by this issue along with infidelity. These two reasons are the major causes of divorce. If one of you is not good at money management, then yield to who is best. In a marriage, there needs to be a budget that is to be adhered to. Savings, life insurance, and retirement plans need to be included in this budget. Also, date night needs to be included. Whatever is not spent needs to be saved. Travel needs to be included. Recreation and self-care need to be included.

The budget needs to reflect your real life and there will be a discussion about decreasing spending in certain areas. Can we make coffee at home rather than spending that money at Starbucks daily? What meals can we prepare at home rather than eating out? What can we do ourselves that we ask others to do? You may decide that the housekeeper and car washes are not optional. You may decide that you want to do your own lawn but is that a good idea? You would need the equipment and spend the time to do it, which requires 3 hours of your time, but only 45 minutes when a service does it. Some decisions need to be made based on those criteria. What are the opportunity costs associated with this activity?

Some couples opt for one joint account and other separate accounts. While others just have two joint accounts—one checking and one saving. Either way, there is still discipline and the same involvement in the decision-making tree. All communication of the plans needs to be written down.

Do not rely on each other's memory for the decisions which you have made. That will be the source of an argument that may not end well.

Money is critical, precious, and a tool to achieve many things. Money earned requires hard work. Mismanagement of that money translates into disrespect for the work which was required to receive that money. The earner may be offended by that disrespect, which will be the cause of strife and anger in your relationship. Resentment also eats away at couples because of unresolved financial issues.

Be honest with yourself and each other so that you can reach an agreement that will lead to a better understanding of your future progress.

NOTES

Notes

QUESTIONS

1. What is your monetary philosophy? Does that align with your mate's philosophy?

___

2. How can you shorten the distance between the philosophies?

___

3. What can you do to change your spending habits?

___

4. What is your savings plan?

___

5. Does your credit need to be repaired? If so, when can you get started?

___

6. Where is your budget? Write it on paper.

7. How much do you spend on frivolous stuff?

8. What do you anticipate your financial issues will be in your marriage?

REFLECTION

BECAUSE I DO

A Successful Second

It may be your second marriage but you need to be focused on making it as if you were never married the first time. Your new mate does not want to hear what happened last time that you were unsuccessfully married.

A successful second is a feat. It was already a miracle that you remarried in the first place. So let's celebrate that first.

You joined in order to live your life together so you both need to be committed to the process of making this work. The statistics are against you so the work will be harder.

Make your mate your best friend and confidant even if the secret is about your mate. You need glue—gorilla strength glue—in order to keep your relationship together. Everything and everyone is against you. Sometimes your worst will be yourself.

You got a second chance at being great. You will need to do two things: (1) do what you wanted and what you should have done in the first marriage; and, (2) don't do what you did wrong in the first marriage. Give it your all! Break the record for best mate ever. Keep focused on the relationship in a way that overwhelms even you. Offer your mate the best version of yourself. Keep your mate first. Make some relationship ground rules. These will help you keep your relationship on a great path.

What is required to make a successful relationship? What does this mean to each of you? That needs to be the first discussion. You need to be honest with each other. This discussion needs to be with notes in order to remind you of what you agreed to.

How did you want to be loved?

What is your love language?

What are your deal breakers?

What is your curfew?

Who else can you travel with?

What locations are off-limits?

BECAUSE I DO

What time is dinner?

How many days each week do you need to have dinner?

What happens to cell phones?

Do you exchange passwords?

How will you manage social media?

How will you raise and discipline current children?

Will there be new children?

How will you deal with each of your ex's?

How will you manage money?

What happens with major purchases?

If your credit is not above 700, what do we need to do to get it there?

Where will you live?

What happens to the other property?

Where do we want to be in one year?

Where do we want to be in five years?

Where do we want to be in ten years?

How will we retire?

Where will we vacation?

Do you have a will?

When will you write one or revise the current one?

There are about a hundred more questions that we can ask each other in order to insure a successful second. The issue is insuring that are honest and transparent so that the path to success is not derailed with lies, half-truths, and inauthentic behavior and information.

Success is the focus. This is not the time to be dishonest or not be forthright about your life and needs.

Make sure that this is the person with whom you will grow old and with whom you will die. Reform from all the attitudes and behaviors of your former self—all-inclusive self. Life will be easier if you just relinquish to the truth.

Your mate wants to trust you and vice versa. What can you do to make sure that trust happens? What went wrong in your last marriage? What are you going to do to change that situation? If the theory that people do not change is true, then that also applies to you. What are you going to do to ensure that the reputation does not persist or continue?

In order to have a successful second, you need to find the errors of your past, make sure that they do not happen again, and then create an environment where your mate loves you, trusts you, and does not lie to you.

This requires characteristics and behavior that you never imagined you will need to exhibit. What do you need to do to make sure that you do just that?

Focus on your marriage.

Pay attention to your spouse.

Listen as your mate speaks.

Plan to meet his needs so that you won't need any attorneys in the near future.

A successful second.

Notes

NOTES

Questions

1. Why did you get divorced?

___

2. Why do you want to remarry?

___

3. Why did you choose your mate?

___

4. What are you going to do to ensure that this is a successful second?

___

5. What are you willing to do to make it last and be viable rather than perfunctory?

___

6. What are your non-negotiables in a relationship?

7. What happens when your non-negotiable(s) is violated?

Reflection

HE STARTED IT

It's her fault.

It's his fault.

She started it.

He's to blame.

Why is there blame? Where is the censorship? Why is the end of most relationships based on who did or did not do something?

In traditional relationships, blame is customary. Relationships are governed by who is right or/and wrong. Based on that, then the 'winner' gets the 'prize.'

Where does that land you? Divorce court? Is someone sleeping on the couch? The silent treatment? If we are solution-oriented instead, then we are better able to solve the blame for a win-win situation for your relationship.

Win-win? That is never heard of in most relationships. Consider the situation first. Is this situation relative to propelling life forward? Let's examine two scenarios: toothpaste tubes versus an empty bank account.

Some couples argue over where the toothpaste tube is squeezed. Some squeeze in the middle. Others squeeze from the end. Some even squeeze it at the tube's opening. Does where you squeeze the toothpaste actually matter? Solution: buy two tubes of toothpaste. Problem solved. No more arguments. If you are arguing about toothpaste and toilet paper, then there is a real issue. You and your mate are not really arguing about those small non-issues.

The empty bank account is based on too much spending and not enough earnings. Overspending is a definite issue between couples when you all are sharing an account. If you spent too much on food, then he cannot buy gas for the car. This is an argument! There is a definite budget management issue that needs to be discussed and decided.

Those are just two extreme examples that are evident in the marriages of all people. The reality is that we are humans with desires and unspoken expectations. The problem is that when two people also have unspoken expectations then there is too much that stands to chance and that also means that those expectations will not be met and this will lead to issues in the relationship. This is counter-productive and actually counter-intuitive.

Blame is not a productive way to spend your time. Blame requires keeping track of the wrongdoings of your mate. Isn't there a better way to spend your time than keeping track of wrongdoings?

Blame is not a productive way to spend your time. Blame requires keeping track of the wrongdoings of your mate. Isn't there a better way to spend time than keeping track of wrongs? These infractions are limited to issues that are not life-threatening or ethically challenging. However, this renders attention required to positively impact the relationship.

Blame is heavy to offer and even harder to receive. Whom do you know that relishes in hearing what they do wrong all of the time? The ideal situation is to be able to share your concerns and determine if they can be remedied. If so, by when? Further, how will your mate upgrade to the new needs? Do you cooperate when these discussions occur?

Blame requires energy that, if directed to the positive parts of the relationship, consider how much peace and happiness you could experience. If you are going to fight, may it lead to an unprecedented closeness and to love the other person greater than you ever thought possible, better than they think they deserve, and more extravagantly than is reasonable. Life is too short for anything else. You deserve to be loved at that level and you deserve to love at that same level of extravagance!

What do you gain by blaming and fighting? What are the real issues? What does the fight solve? Do you even resolve the issues about which you argue? Are you really serious about holding that grudge, keeping that 'wrong' alive, reminding each other of mistakes, and committing to unforgiveness?

That is a recipe for relationship disaster. You are to blame. You are equally to blame for the issues in your relationship because both of you could have fixed the issues but chose to let them continue to foster and remain unresolved.

You will have to resolve how you will stop blaming and start resolving and create a space to forgive and never mention it again. You will also need to make sure that you do not cause that same issue again. You will also need to live and love like it never happened.

NOTES

Notes

Questions

1. Is it who you are or is it who you are not that causes these fights?
   _____
   _____
   _____

2. What are you gaining from these fights?
   _____
   _____
   _____

3. What happens if you are fighting so that you can go see another person? How do you stop doing that?
   _____
   _____
   _____

4. What would make the fighting stop?
   _____
   _____
   _____

5. When did fighting become more important than loving your mate?
   _____
   _____

6. How can you begin to stop arguing and start talking about the issues as well as resolving the actual issues?

REFLECTION

BECAUSE I DO

FIGHTING FAIR

When you pick a fight, pick one which leads you to love another person greater person than you ever possible, better than they think they deserve, and more extravagantly than is even reasonable. Life is too short for anything else. You deserve to be loved at that level and you deserve to love at that same level of extravagance.

Remember, you all will create the rules together. Below, you will find a list of suggestions:

- Don't go to bed angry.
- Listen before requiring to be heard.
- Listen before offering a solution.
- Don't get mad if your mate does not use your suggestion—it was a suggestion.
- The past should remain in the past on both sides:
  - ☐ Don't bring up the past.
  - ☐ Don't do the things which cause your mate to remember the past.
- Equal thinking time:
  - ☐ If you pondered that information for three days, then your mate should be afforded that same time period.
- Ask yourself if this matters in the grand scheme of your relationship and your life.
- Previous hurts or transgressions are off-limits.
- No insults.
- Keep your business to yourself. When you share your arguments with family, you fail to come back and share the reconciliation with the same urgency.
- Ask for forgiveness.
- Apologize when you are wrong.
- Remember when you fight that you love this person. Don't say anything that you will regret and causes them to question your love for them.
- Remain calm.
- Speak slowly.
- Be respectful.
- Don't fight in your bedroom.

Fighting fair is not difficult. It is based on respect and love. Fighting fair is important because you desire to preserve your relationship.

Arguments or disagreements turn into fights because of power—not usually about the actual issue. What is really worth arguing about? Irresponsible spending? Yes. Infidelity, both physical and emotional? Yes. Entering into large financial commitments without agreement? Yes. Are the dishes not being washed? Not so much. Who didn't take the trash out? No. Who didn't cook dinner? Not really.

When those issues become arguments and then a full-fledged fight by whatever definition you use, then there is an underlying issue.

When your mate wants to fight uncharacteristically then please start with the real issue. Find out what the real issue is. Be patient. The issue is obviously something that your mate is not ready to share or doesn't know how to address.

What is the real issue? How will you find out what the real issue is? How do you start with the real issue so that you and your mate can reach a solution and agreement?

Fighting is also about trust. When did you stop trusting your mate's judgment? Or their decision-making skills? When did they start making poor financial choices? Fights come from a place of deep resentment. What happened? Was it always this way and was just overlooked? Or is this new? And if so, why?

What does a solution look like that meets the needs and expectations of both of you? Can you reach a resolution? Is it possible to make a decision that is equitable and neither of you feels like you lost? Is one person compromising more? Does that build resentment?

Is that possible? Can you do it? Can you overlook the nature of the fight in order to see behind the smokescreen to reach the actual issue? Fights usually divide a couple. Defy the norm and use the 'fights' to grow closer. Seek to understand the mate at his/her point of need. Listen with your heart, rather than your mind. What is your mate's mind on? What is really going on? Your mate needs your attention. Your mate needs your heart and your compassion. Find out why your mate wants to fight.

How to reach a resolution:

1. Try touching and fighting. If you can touch and continue to fight, then the argument will not be as volatile as when you are at a distance.

2. Introduce the issue. Then take a break and return to the matter. Once you return to the argument or issue, you should return focused on the actual matter, rather than the emotional details which infiltrate the matter.
3. Write down what the actual issues are so that the focus is on the facts, rather than emotionally driven.
4. For more serious matters, schedule a mediator.

These are some options, but you need to choose the best option for your family. Each issue needs a different method to resolve.

The issue needs to be separate from your personal relationship. The best part of your relationship is that you can keep these details separate.

Fighting fair is a skill and a necessary one at best. Fighting fair will help with maintaining a healthy relationship.

The comfort of knowing that you can disgrace and not wreck your relationship while trying to resolve your situation. End each discussion with a hug and maybe even a kiss.

Fighting fair is essential.

Notes

NOTES

QUESTIONS

1. What will your rules be?

   _____
   _____
   _____

2. How do you determine what is important enough to argue about?

   _____
   _____
   _____

3. Is there any argument or topic which could end your marriage? Does your mate know this?

   _____
   _____
   _____

4. Who do you know who fights fairly? Can they help you to do the same?

   _____
   _____
   _____

5. What of what you have learned can you share with others?

   _____
   _____

6. How will this improve and enhance your relationship?

Reflection

SEX: PUT IT ON HER MIND

Your wives are not having sex with you! You want sex. You want to have sex with your wife. So here is a hint: Put it on her mind! How do you do that? How do you put sex on her mind without seeming pushy or insensitive? How do you make her want sex with you the same way that you do?

When you think about sex, what do you do to share that desire with her? Do you send a text? Do you call? And mention it in casual conversation?

You have to introduce the idea before you get home. Start early so that she can plan her day so that she will be willing and available to engage you.

One of the things that you need to fix is your everything. Imagine a wife with 3 boys and from the time she arrives home after work, she is chasing and corralling these boys. She feeds them. She cooked that meal. She cleans the kitchen while they play. She takes them upstairs for a bath. She dresses them. She reads them bedtime stories and puts them to bed.

At 9 pm, she is exhausted. She has not stopped moving since she put her feet on the floor at 5:30 am.

You arrived home at 6 pm. You ate. You watched television. At 9 pm, when she comes to your bedroom, you are ready to be intimate and close. She rejects you because she is tired. She falls asleep.

Does this sound familiar? If so, then you need to make some adjustments. Consider the divide and conquer approach. How about you bathe, read, and put them in bed? Excuse her to your room so that she can bathe and refresh so that she will feel like making love to you. Does that sound doable? Have you ever considered that? How many days each week can you do that? Do you think it would make a difference in your relationship?

She works just like you. She has stress just like you. She has dreams, hopes, and goals—just like you do. She has needs as well but she puts all of her personal interests aside so that her family has all that they need. Keep that in mind when you complain that she does not let you touch her.

Further, complete your list of items that she needs around the house in the next 10 days. All of the repairs, upgrades, and maintenance—complete it all in the next ten days. That act may immediately increase your sexual activity. If that does not help you, then it still needed to be done.

Compliments and encouragement also influence her desires. Flowers and trinkets may help if she likes that. Give her more of you and you will see that same attention in return.

Consider what changed: did she ever initiate sex? Does she like sex? What does she like about sex? Does she feel comfortable with her body? Does she view herself as sexy? Do you view her as sexy? If so, does she know it? If not, help her to return to sexy for both of you.

Be honest with her and help her to be honest with you. Talk about sex and the frequency that you desire. Get her feedback. Did it change from when you were dating? Courting? If so, what happened? Did it change after the kids were born? If so, then her body experienced some hormonal changes with her libido. What are you willing to do to get that back? What would she do for you if this was in the reverse?

Sex is an exciting, but sensitive topic. It does need some delicate engineering. As a married couple, you vowed to be there for each other. Flirt with her on texts, email, and video service. Remember to make her feel special. Rewind the time when you could not wait to see each other and craved each other's company.

There are many reasons why she does not think about sex, so help her to think about it. Entice her to want to and make it amazing.

Put it on her mind.

NOTES

Notes

Questions

1. How will you put it on her mind?

   _____
   _____
   _____

2. What is your plan to move forward?

   _____
   _____
   _____

3. Plan a talk with her. Write down what you plan to say. rehearse this with a female family member or friend. Revise based on her feedback.

   _____
   _____
   _____

4. What was your ah-ha moment?

   _____
   _____
   _____

5. When you asked her about the new plan, what did she say?

   _____
   _____
   _____

Reflection

Your Time Counts:
Put the Remote Down

You are at this conference because she asked you to go and you needed to go. Relationships will have challenges but you can mitigate the damage by considering the time that you spend or don't spend with your wife. Your time edifies her. She needs to hear your voice, feel your sigh on her neck, feel your heartbeat, hear your cough, taste your breath, and feel your arms.

She needs the same amount of time that she needed when she met you. Marriage is often treated like a box we check. Rather, marriage is a living, breathing mechanism which needs nurture and care, maintenance and reorganizing. Please know that she needs your touch and your energy.

There is a truck driver with a wife and four children. He drives from 7 am to 9 pm every day. One day he felt that she did not like him anymore. He sought a counselor who told him that his wife still liked and loved him. She had four children with him. He needed to understand that she is talking to him daily. That means that she is still engaged in the relationship.

The counselor suggested that he email or text her every day asking her what was on her mind. He would be able to address all of her concerns and when he got home they would be able to spend their limited time together on just the two of them—to reconnect, to revive, to renew, and to refresh their relationship.

He was amazed at the results of that advice. They only had about 30-45 minutes every day to spend together. They need to use that time wisely, rather than on household management, and other issues.

Consider your relationship. What has your wife been asking for? What does she need? What does she crave from you? What did you formerly do for her that you might need to reintroduce in order to reconnect with your wife?

What are you all missing? When is your date night? Do you eat dinner together? When is your next vacation together?

As you consider these questions, you need to develop some answers which lead to a plan. When was the last time you held hands? Do you still hug? Who lets go first when you hug? Do you still spoon in bed? Do you caress her like you handle and protect that remote?

Most wives envy the remote because you hold it more than you hold her. You give that television time that that she would appreciate having. She needs that time with you to affirm her, to embrace her, to share with her, to engage her, to problem-solve with her, and so much more.

This is a new century, a new era. Long gone are the days when women feel that they need to stay unhappily married. Your grandmothers never considered divorce no matter what your grandfather did or did not do. That generation needed a man and was taught to never leave that man. This generation was not taught that. They will divorce and walk away because they are not fulfilled and satisfied. Consider that she needs and wants you but that must be mutual.

Protect her time with you. Ask her how she wants to spend days with you.

Dance in your living room to youtube.com or Alexa. Watch her favorite movie for the tenth time. Plan a picnic in the park, patio, or living room. Do something for her that will amaze her. Book a vacation to her dream location.

Make her smile again. You have the influence to get her to laugh and forgive, smile, and blush.

If you have been unfaithful, the second issue is that you gave someone else time that you previously said you didn't have. How did you find time for another woman? There is so much that she wishes you would give her.

Please understand that your time is valuable to her. She should be able to count on your time. Why can't you give her your time? Willingly? Graciously? Without her having to beg and bargain?

This time that you keep from her may be the very wedge that has stifled your growth in this relationship.

You have the power to stop this path. Also, share with her your sports interests as well as teach her as necessary.

This is not a comfortable situation for either of you. You owe her the time that she requested. She needs your time like you need air—it is her oxygen!

How would you feel if she never had time for you? Well, that is how she feels, and ten times worse. Just spend time with her. Remember the statement about this generation's woman. They are also independent and self—sufficient. This is important because when she gets transparent before you, then you need to be able to receive that and respond appropriately. Asking you about time together is her being vulnerable before you. She wants to feel wanted and your time spent with her affirms her; that will reassure her that she is still important to you.

Spend time with your spouse.

Put down the remote.

Notes

NOTES

QUESTIONS

1. What is the reason that she cannot get your time? Your undivided attention?

   _____

   _____

   _____

2. Plan the next 6 Fridays/Saturdays for your date nights.

   _____

   _____

   _____

   _____

   _____

   _____

3. Plan the dream vacation for the two of you.

   _____

   _____

   _____

   _____

   _____

   _____

4. What nights are you committed to eating dinner together?

5. When was the last time you hugged? How can you increase this?

6. When was the last time you held hands? How can you increase this?

7. When was the last time you kissed deeply? How can you increase this?

8. When was the last time you made love? How can you increase this?

9. When was the last time you spooned? How can you increase this?

10. What will you do to change the course?

11. What does she want from you?

12. What does she crave from you?

13. What does she need from you?

Reflection

BECAUSE I DO

Treat Her Like the Mistress

This does not imply that you have ever had a mistress. Let's look at how the mistress is treated. She had dedicated and planned time set aside just for the two of you uninterrupted. The mistress vacations in great places that you planned and prepared for. You rendezvous and she feels special. She does not get the excuses that you give your wife.

This time is QUALITY; planned and protected. You are strategic. You are planning. You are intentional. You are purposed. You are focused.

What happened if you treated your wife like the mistress? How would that make her feel? Would it bring the two of you closer? When was the last time that you surprised her? When was the last time an evening out was your idea?

If any of these answers is no then you should start to improve that behavior. Treat her well because you chose her and she accepted. This is the role that you signed up for—this is your job. Do you find it hard to match her energy? Is she a planner? Does she like romance and romantic events?

This takes us back to communication. Are you texting her with flirtatious statements and sexy emojis? Are you sending her a picture of yourself even though you saw her before you left home? Are you inviting her to the rendezvous spots spontaneously? Are you using your points and miles for a romantic getaway just because?

What about talking on the phone on the way home? These are things men do when they have mistresses, so you need to do it for your wife.

You are trying to keep the romance alive and to draw closer to each other.

It is almost guaranteed that if you do any of these things you will win her over. If you do half of them, then you will be in the husband hall of fame. Your intention is to infuse more intimacy into your relationship.

The concept sounded scary, even crazy, but imagine if you did treat her like the mistress so that she would fall in love all over again.

Notes

NOTES

QUESTIONS

1. What are you going to do to bring your wife closer to you?

   _____
   _____
   _____

2. Is she upset with you that this would cure?

   _____
   _____
   _____

3. Is she worth your effort? What does it require to make that effort?

   _____
   _____
   _____

4. Based on what you knew about mistresses, what can do to improve your relationship with the suggestions that were provided to you?

   _____
   _____
   _____

5. Do you need as list or some assistance with developing and executing a plan?

   _____
   _____

REFLECTION

BECAUSE I DO

Be a Better Husband Without Changing a Thing

You are a great husband! You are a wonderful man! Being consistently that husband is hard work but not difficult. It requires you to be the same. She wants to be you to be the same man she fell in love with. She fell in love with your conversation, your flirting, your attentiveness, and your presence. You once invited her into your space but at some point, you excused her from that same space. Giving her what she needs makes you a great husband. You usually make two errors: (1) you give her time to someone else, (2) you don't respond appropriately when she asks you about it. You are still able to talk, flirt, spoil, and be present so do it and she will give you everything you want.

Being a great husband means that you are dedicated to your wife. She needs to be number one so that she can feel like the wife that she is, rather than the doormat she says she feels like. What can you do about that?

She needs to know she is the only one. If there is a history of infidelity, then this is important to do. There may be some concern at the back of her mind. Please understand she is still hurt, although it diminishes each day as long as she does not see any additional signs of that returning.

Are you all happy? Is she happy? Are you happy? Do you want to improve your relationship? If you do, then put aside your regular lifestyle and make the big gesture—the big move.

Can you do the THING that she has always wanted? What would it cost you? What would you gain?

Being a better husband is quite the feat. It requires listening, loving, forgiveness, attentiveness, flirting, presence, and patience. Communication is also a part of being a great husband. She needs to be a great wife and communicate as well.

What do you need from her to be a great husband? What do you need from her to be a great wife? When she fell in love with you, you were a different man, but that difference is she does not know all of this new man that you have grown into. Why isn't she welcomed in your space anymore? What are you doing? What are you hiding?

She needs and wants the man that she fell in love with even though our growth and changes. You need to be committed to her and your relationship. What changed? What happened? When will it be corrected?

When will you initiate closeness between the two of you? She craves that closeness. She craves your attentiveness. She yearns for your flirting. She needs your presence. Your conversation is her oxygen. Give her all of you again.

NOTES

Notes

QUESTIONS

1. What has changed about you since before you were married?

2. What has changed about you since you have been married?

3. What will you need in order to revive the flirting, conversations, and attentiveness?

4. What can you do in order to become more present?

5. How do you support your wife in the areas of her life?

6. Why did you get married?

7. Do you still want to be married? If no, what can you do in order to want to be married to your wife?

Reflection

BECAUSE I DO

Act Like the Husband

The husband has a job description. Be supportive. Be loving. Be her audience. Be engaged. Be present. Be faithful. Be a sounding board. Be a handyman. Be attentive. Be spectacular. Be sparkle guy. Be a little protective. Be a friend. Be a provider. Be fun. Be spontaneous. Be neat. Be her strong tower.

Address her needs. Get to know her again and again. She just wants to be able to depend on you like you promised that you would. There is a change in this modern-aged woman. This new woman does not accept the men of the past. Our moms and grandmothers accepted circumstances and situations, which new women do not accept in the same manner.

Our fathers and grandfathers were missing in action, fathering more children than they were willing to share with us, had affairs, and neglected time with us.

We want a better man than they were to our mothers and grandmothers. We want a man who can be true and loyal, dedicated and committed to us and only us.

Some men feel that men should be able to cheat and see other women without consequence. That is the world that women find unacceptable. Your wife should not have to turn the other way and just be okay with you having a mistress or some other women that you make time to spend with while you neglect her and tell her that you are busy.

The husband that she needs and wants is one that does not take her for granted, does not seek comfort from others, and lies to her by making promises that you never intend to keep.

Please do what you signed up to do: Act like and Be the Husband!

Notes

NOTES

QUESTIONS

1. What did you expect from your marriage?
   _____
   _____

2. Why did you get married?
   _____
   _____

3. Do you feel that you are a good husband? Why do you feel that way?
   _____
   _____

4. What does your wife need from you?
   _____
   _____

5. What will you do to meet those needs?
   _____
   _____

6. What are you willing to do to save or revive your marriage?

_____

_____

_____

7. When will you start?

_____

_____

_____

Reflection

Afterword:
A Working Marriage

When you got married, you had blissful plans and hopes. The happiness in marriage ranges from already moved out to we cannot wait to see each other. The investment in another person is what marriage is based on. The quality of your marriage is your responsibility. We are hoping that your marriage will be healthier because you are here today. Please invest in your marriage at an all-time high.

This relationship does not take breaks. It does not have any brakes. It does not have a vacation clause. It does not have a time-out corner. It is full-time, hard work that makes us love each other more. The work makes us stronger as a couple and an individual.

How will you make your marriage work? How will you edify your mate? How will you go the extra mile for your mate? How will assist your mate with the dreams that you have dreamed? How will meet the needs of the other person? How will you learn to share with your mate?

What is the best part of your relationship? What is the best part of you? What is the best part of your mate? What is the best part of your intimacy? What is the worst part of those same elements? This is the basis of the value of the relationship. The objective is that the marriage is a working and living and breathing element which means that it is viable and alive and well.

Everything that is worth having is worth working for. This is the element that needs some recognition: your marriage is worth having so it is worth working for.

This marriage thing is not for the quitter or the faint at heart. It is for those who have hope, and perseverance. It is for those who do not quit. For those with respect for boundaries and singularity. It is for those of us who can't wait to make another person happy and who genuinely want to see the other person succeed in everything that the mate wishes to achieve.

Love extravagantly is two of the move powerful words which once together, those two words are superfluous! But most importantly, behavior makes a huge difference in the world.

A great marriage is a working marriage!

BECAUSE I DO

Resources

Love letter writing pages	168
Book and counseling resources	171
About the Conference	173
Acknowledgments	181
About the Former and Future Bride	183

My Love Letter

Because I Do

Book and Counseling Resources

The Five Love Languages by Dr. Gary Chapman
Married Roommates by Allen Wagner
The Sex-Starved Marriage: A Couple's Guide to Boosting Their Marriage Libido
Woulda. Coulda. Shoulda.: A Divorce Coach's Guide to Staying Married by Jennifer Hurvitz
I Love You But I Don't Trust You by Mira Kirshenbaum
Talk to Me Like I am Someone You Love by Nancy Dreyfus
From Two to One: The Notebook for the Christian Couple by Minister Onedia N. Gage
Getting Away to Get It Together by Bill and Carolyn Wellons
The Love Dare by Alex and Stephen Kendrick
Saving Your Marriage Before It Starts by Drs. Les and Leslie Parrott
Questions Couples Ask by Drs. Les and Leslie Parrott
Powerful Promises for Every Couple by Jim and Elizabeth George
The Christian Husband by Bob Lepine
Kingdom Man by Tony Evans
Kingdom Woman by Tony Evans
The Power of a Praying Wife by Stormie Omartian
The Power of a Praying Husband by Stormie Omartian
The Power of Prayer to Change Your Marriage by Stormie Omartian
The Excellent Wife by Martha Peace
The Excellent Husband by Martha Peace
40 Unforgettable Dates with Your Mate by Dr. Gary and Barbara Rosberg
When God Writes Your Love Story by Eric and Leslie Ludy
Love and Respect by Emerson Eggerichs

Movies
The Longest Ride
The Story of Us
We Bought a Zoo
Hope Springs
Best Man Holiday
Shall We Dance
Jerry MacGuire
It's Complicated
Fireproof

BECAUSE I DO

Sweet Home Alabama
The Women
Mr. & Mrs. Smith
The Notebook
War Room
Jumping the Broom
Something to Talk About
The Devil Loves Prada
A Thousand Words
Love and Basketball
The Blind Side
 50 Shades Darker
Creed 2
The Other Woman
Up Close & Personal
The Vow

About the Conference
Because I Do: A Working Marriage
Conference Agenda

7:45   Check In

8:00   Opening Session

8:30   Panel Discussion

9:30   Workshop Session One

10:30   Workshop Session Two

11:30   Keynote lecture: Changing A Legacy, Leaving A Legacy
            Lunch

12:30   Love Letter Composition

1:00   Women's General Session
          Men's General Session

3:00   Love Letter Sharing

3:30   Workshop Session Three

4:30   Workshop Session Four

5:30   Closing

6:00   Dismissal

Because I Do: A Working Marriage Workshop Descriptions

Workshop Session One

Marriage vs. Technology

Does your mate complain about your phone usage, Facebook or Twitter? Then you could be having a problem with your technology. Technology is interrupting your relationship. This interruption could be just irritation or it could cause distrust to start. This can be overcome. Let us share with you how to manage your technology without creating disease in your relationship.

Equip Your Mate to be Successful

You and your mate chose each other: act like it. You will tell EVERYONE including the postmaster that your mate messed up and how they messed up and what they should do to fix it. EXCEPT for your mate! What stops us from equipping the very person you lay down with each night and with whom you share your bills? Let's talk about that process and problem.

Communication=Intimacy

Is what you are not willing to share hurting your relationship? Communication equals intimacy! Your intimacy should be cultivated with healthy verbal discussions, texting, email, webcams, and other available mechanisms. Let's be clear that you two got together through communicative means. If you have stopped that then you should consider how to restart that dialogue. Your relationship is worth some conversation.

How to Save Your Marriage

This is the hardest point: saving your marriage. The first step is to decide you want this marriage. The four additional steps will be discussed in the session. This is a powerful class led by a couple who have been married for a couple of decades. They have survived several issues which would dismantle average marriages. Saving your marriage starts with you.

The Five Love Languages

This book by Dr. Gary Chapman covers the dynamics of your love language and how to share that love language, along with managing your mate's love language. This is a powerful tool for your marriage. The ability to love someone in their language is a powerful mechanism to enhance your love and relationship.

She (He) Started It

The other person is always to blame because we are so great as a partner. I am sure that each person would agree that that is the case. Or maybe not.

Great Relationships

Great relationships are defined differently by each person in that relationship. Within the same relationship, the two people have different relationship definitions. Whether aligned and alike or not, they are both important. The next part is to work on those definitions. Consider your relationship similar to your job. You go to work daily. You manage others, solve the world's issues, and make millions for yourself or someone else however when you get home, you go on vacation, or into hibernation. In essence, you have quit your relationship. Great relationships require WORK. Work requires TIME. Time requires PRESENCE: physically, emotionally, and spiritually.

Workshop Session Two

The Spiritual Diet

What does your marriage require from you spiritually? Should you pray over her daily? Should you pray for him daily? Should you attend church together weekly? Should you fast together on big issues within your lives? What does your marriage require? These and other topics will be covered for the spiritual wellness of your relationship.

Forgiveness is Critical

To forgive is divine. Marriage is no place for a grudge. The marriage needs much forgiveness, willingly, daily. This is the foundation with marriages require. Forgive with a grateful spirit. This is the grace that we all need to survive each day.

Restoration of Trust

Something happened. Someone was unfaithful. Someone lied. Someone is selfish. Someone is secretive. The outcome is a lack of trust. This is the reason for a relationship—someone to trust and "put your stuff down." This has changed. You do not trust and do not ever intend to. But that will kill your marriage. How do I trust him again? How do I trust her again? This workshop will start the dialogue and make some healthy suggestions for how to maneuver through the lack of trust.

A Successful Second

Well, you are married for the second time, so now what? How do we avoid the statistics about second marriages and still focus on each other? We will share tips and our testimonies about making the second marriage work and maybe even better than the first. We will include a discussion about blended families.

An Amicable Divorce

If you decide to divorce, do so in an amicable manner. This workshop will be led by an attorney who will share the details of divorce and will answer as many general questions as possible. The workshop is designed to give you an honest look at how this really works so that you can make objective decisions rather than ones based on emotions.

Fighting Fair

Let's just take this one issue at a time. We have fighting rules. Yes, rules. As a couple, we will create them together and hold each other accountable for keeping them in play so that reasonable outcomes can take place. The rules could say we do not go to bed angry or we take a time out and we come back together when cooler heads prevail. Whatever the rules are, we will adhere to them as well as use them to build our relationships.

Money Makes a Difference

Well she spends too much on shoes too often and he golfs every week, but we cannot afford a family vacation. Let's talk about money and its ramifications in our marriages.

Workshop Sessions Three and Four

Women Only

You are the Companion

Based on several research sources, including William Farley's <u>His Needs, Her Needs</u>, the man's second biggest need is his wife as a companion. He is peacock proud when his wife shows up on his arm at the craziest events—where other women decline to attend. He is proud because you are there. No big mystery or guesswork is needed. He just wants you there. We will discuss how to navigate these scenarios and how to find your place in these settings where you may be technically out of place.

Are You Sexy?

Are you sexy? To yourself? To others? To him? The only answer that matters is his, however, you have to be sexy to yourself so that you can be sexy to him. We will discuss the elements to enhance your sexy, define your sexy and increase your sex appeal to him. When you are sexy to him, then the relationship is different and has a different context.

Womanhood Defined: Proverbs 31:10-31

Woman, you have a job. We will dissect the scriptures and apply them to this century. We will advocate for each other and how to be successful within that role. The conversation will be intense however the outcome will be liberating.

What Did You Just Say? Your Communication Counts

Did you just hear the words that came out of your mouth? Did you just disrespect him and yourself? Did you just love him out loud? We are investigating the words and tone we use and how that will inspire or instigate the relationship we are in. This is the time to deal with communication from your view and investigate how that sounded to him. The challenge is that we are new millennia women with independent ideas while married to an old-school man who will not admit it. How do you communicate with him and move mountains at the same time?

Sexyssentials!

We are going to do the following things: stop faking it, stop holding it hostage, and keep the bedroom on fire. These sex topics are essential for your marriage. Let's talk about SEX!

Men Only

Sex: Put it on her mind

I have heard that your wives are not having sex with you! I understand that you want sex. I know that you want to have sex with your wife. So I have a hint: put it on her mind! How do you put it on her mind? How do you persuade her to want to have SEX? With You? She does not think about sex as you do. She is thinking about taking care of you and your family and all that it entails. We will coach you about putting it on her mind in a manner in which she will want to cooperate and participate.

Your Time Counts: Put The Remote Down

If you want to love your wife and you are confused about why she is not talking, put down the remote. If you use her glasses to see yourself, it may not be all that you think it is. Consider the remote and how you touch it and hold it and never let anyone else touch it and hold it. You possess it. Do you give your wife that type of attention? No. But she needs it. Give her that time. Put the remote down and give her your time. Let ESPN go for one afternoon and check the pulse of your wife and relationship.

Treat Her Like the Mistress

When I first made this statement, my friends laughed nervously and then asked me what did I mean? If you treated your wife or your girlfriend like you treat the mistress, your relationship would be great. The mistress gets the prime time with your plans. You plan for her and the time is QUALITY. You make rendezvous plans strategically and you spend choice time with her. The wife/GF gets the leftover time but you want prime-time results. Call your wife/GF. Arrange to meet her in quaint places. Cancel the excuses for why you don't date or pamper your wife. Make yourself available to her like she was the mistress. Watch your relationship change.

Be a Better Husband Without Changing a Thing

You are a great husband! You are a wonderful man! I recently complimented someone by telling him he was a wonderful man and he is. And so are you. Being consistently that husband is hard work but not difficult. It requires you to be the same. She wants you to be the same man she fell in love with. She fell in love with your conversation, your flirting, your attentiveness, and your presence. You once invited her into your space but at some point, you excused her from that same space. Giving her what she needs makes you a great husband. You usually make two errors: (1) you give her time to someone/something else, and, (2) you don't respond appropriately when she asks you about it. You are still able to talk, flirt, spoil and be present so do it and she will give you everything you want.

Act Like the Husband

Do the work required of the husband so that you can keep your job. The average woman is not going to accept the mediocrity her father gave her mother, so likewise you need to consider the needs of your wife so that you are not living with or divorcing a stranger. This is quite direct and maybe even harsh, however, we need to consider that she needs you or she would not have married you. Do your job!

BECAUSE I DO

Acknowledgments

God, thank You for Your plans for me. Thank You for **Because I Do: A Working Marriage** and for choosing me to complete Your project. I just want to please You. Thank You for continuing to anoint me and to invest in me and my gifts, which keep surprising me. Thank You for loving and forgiving me.

Jordan and Nehemiah, thank you for supporting me and my endeavors. Thank you for loving me, especially when I do nothing without a pen and a clipboard, thank you for enduring my late nights, your ideas, the sounding board, the love, and the support. Thank you for celebrating our legacy.

To my prayer partners and my accountability partners, thank you for the long talks, the powerful prayers, and the encouragement. To my pastor and church family, thank you so much for your love and support.

BECAUSE I DO

Onedia N. Gage seeks to share her outlandish pursuit of life with her love ethic. She desires to share her advice with you in a manner that helps you do the same through her example. She hopes that these words will motivate you.

Please feel free to contact me and share your progress.
onediagage@onedia... , or @onediangage (twitter).
www.onediagespe...

Blogtalkradio.com/onediagage

Youtube.com/onediagage

Facebook.com/onediagage

Because I Do

Coach ♦ Advocate ♦ Teacher ♦ Facilitator
Conference Speaker ♦ Workshop Leader

To invite Dr. Gage to speak at your school, business, or organization,

Please contact us at: www.onediagespeaks.com

@onediangage (twitter) ♦ onediagage@onediagespeaks.com ♦ facebook.com/onediagage

youtube.com/onediagage ♦ blogtalkradio.com/onediagage ♦ ongage (Instagram)

BECAUSE I DO

Publishing

Do you have a book you want to write, but do not know what to do?

Do you have a book you need to publish but do not know how to start?

Would publishing move your career forward?

Let us help

onediagage@purpleink.net ♦ www.purpleink.net

281.740.5143 ♦ 713.705.5530

www.ingramcontent.com/pod-product-compliance
Lightning Source LLC
Chambersburg PA
CBHW081744100526
44592CB00015B/2294